The Dialogue Based Strategy

A Nonviolent Strategy For Dialogue That Is Aware

By

Dr Howard peck

TABLE OF CONTENTS

ABOUT THE BOOK

An instruction manual for peaceful dialogue to develop more profound and intelligent conversations: Find your voice, speak the truth, and pay close attention.

We spend a lot of time talking to one another, but how much of that time is spent on autopilot, relying on established patterns, and hoping for the best? Can we respectfully listen to others' perspectives and voice our own without having to defend or criticize the other person?

The techniques used by Dialogue Based Strategy will let you:

Speak with assurance; focus on the crucial elements of a conversation; pay attention to what others genuinely worry about; Reduce your anxiety before and during difficult conversations; Find nutrition-inconsistent interactions.

Unconscious communication patterns contribute to the violence and misunderstanding loops ubiquitous in our culture and tear apart our interpersonal connections. We learn to talk and listen with presence, courage, and an open heart, thanks to steven john lectures and practices. He accomplishes this with great precision and comprehension.

REVIEW

Unconscious communication habits not only cause division in our personal relationships, but they also feed into the violence and miscommunication cycles that are pervasive in our society. Howard peck gives teachings and practices that enable us to speak and listen with presence, boldness, and an open heart with clarity and tremendous insight. Radical Acceptance and True Refuge

Dr Howard peck provides us with a masterful blending of concentrated presence and artistic engagement. His leadership will be beneficial to our relationships at work, home, and in other settings. Emotional Intelligence and Altered Traits author Daniel GolemanThis current and compelling book "shows us how compassion, curiosity, and connection can improve people's lives, even in the face of aggressiveness. It is full of practical exercises that create powerful communication and mindfulness skills." —Susan Kaiser Greenland, the writer of The Mindful Child and Mindful Games.

By the time we reach adulthood, the majority of us have developed language and behavioral habits that are so firmly ingrained that prejudice, projection, and assumption are almost a part of every communication we have. It makes sense why we frequently feel so alone and alone. In order to teach us how to reconnect with one another, Dr Howard skillfully combines his mindfulness practice with the NVC concepts. This is a potent manual for genuine and thoughtful thinking, speaking, and listening.

Dialogue based strategy

ABOUT AUTHOR

At retreat facilities and academic institutions across the United States, Dr Howard peck conducts retreats and workshops on mindful communication and meditation. He is a Somatic Experiencing Practitioner, a Certified Trainer of Nonviolent Communication, and a member of the Spirit Rock Teacher's Council. He has a degree in Comparative Religion from American University and instructs in the Insight Meditation community. Howard develops mindfulness training courses for a variety of businesses.

INTRODUCTION

WHAT DOES IT MEAN FOR ME? GAIN USEFUL KNOWLEDGE TO IMPROVE YOUR SPEECH

Like every other person on earth, you have probably encountered the influence that words may have. In difficult times, they may be the factor that makes or destroys a relationship or may mean the difference between giving up and discovering new hope. Our communication with others around us is fundamentally influenced by the words we use and the way we say them.

Dialogue based strategy

CHAPTER 1:

CREATING COMPREHENSION VIA AWARENESS IS THE KEY TO EFFECTIVE COMMUNICATION.

Have you ever talked to someone and they just didn't seem to hear you? Have you ever tried discussing something with a partner whose eyes are riveted to the TV or recounting a story to a buddy whose attention is fixed on his phone? If so, you'll understand how annoying it may be when you're speaking the same language yet nobody seems to be paying attention to you or your words; it's as if you're not even there.

In the end, it means that during certain times, communication is both impossible and impossible.

The main point here is: awareness is the first step to effective communication.

Although it might seem obvious, we rarely pause to consider why we are even speaking in the first place. The response? One word sums it all up: understanding. All communication is done in the hopes of being understood.

But awareness is necessary for comprehension to be the ultimate goal of our conversation. But in terms of communication, what does awareness mean?

The only thing required is your presence.Being physically aware of and perceiving all facets of oneself through your body is more than just a state of consciousness. It involves being aware of your emotional experiences and mental states as they manifest physically.

Most of us may easily practice presence for a brief period by simply shifting our attention inside and becoming aware of our current feelings and experiences.

Maintaining that awareness, particularly when you're having a conversation, is more difficult.

There are valid explanations for this: One thing is that it takes time and effort to let go of our old communication habits, which may include things like shouting at someone when we don't feel like they've been heard or giving them the right treatment. Even when we are aware that these unproductive strategies ineffective, it can be challenging to replace them with positive

approaches to living.

CHAPTER 2:

EFFECTIVE COMMUNICATION STARTS WITH THE FUNDAMENTAL RULE OF LEADING WITH PRESENCE.

Consider the last time you had a swim in the ocean, a moment of closeness with a close friend, or the beauty of a sunset. We feel entirely awake and present during these great, powerful experiences, and we are. They are so wealthy because of that.

But being present has other advantages as well. The ability to be present is something we have access to all the time, not just on those remarkable occasions.

Once mastered, it can help us build lasting relationships and improve our ability to communicate with others.

The main point here is: effective communication is based on the fundamental idea of leading with presence.

So how do we make our talks more present?

Let's start by keeping in mind that presence is all about awareness. It starts with awareness of the present situation without judgment or response.

Starting by considering what you currently know about it, you can utilize a straightforward method to hone your capacity for being present.

Consider what keeps you connected and what keeps you distracted as you work toward your goal. When you slow down, listen to your favorite music, and spend time with close friends, for instance, you may find that you become more conscious of the world around you as well as of yourself. On the other hand, conditions like hunger, fatigue, or stress might cause us to become disengaged. That is what takes place when, for instance, you discover yourself rushing around and dropping things or getting angry and snapping at people. When we lack presence, both communication and, most significantly, our capacity to get things done suffer. However, once you are aware of the factors that hinder connection, you may recognize them in your daily life and take the required steps to address them.

Most importantly, presence entails being authentic and truthful with oneself. That doesn't entail accepting everything that happens or bluntly expressing our opinions. It just entails recognizing and embracing the truth of the situation.

In this manner, it will be simpler for you to recognize when you are becoming agitated or stressed out and to reflect on it. Even if those emotional states can't always be stopped from arising, being aware of them provides you with an option on how to respond. Additionally, by exercising more restraint in your responses, you'll be able to prevent pointless fights.

CHAPTER 3:

MEANINGFUL DISCUSSION DEPENDS ON KNOWING WHEN TO SPEAK AND WHEN TO LISTEN.

A meditation instructor once asked a group of convicts to calculate the total amount of time they had spent there; the total was well over a hundred years. He asked next, "How long did it take you to decide to commit the crime that got you into this situation?" Less than four minutes were spent in total. Such a difference, huh?

Even if the majority of our impulses aren't always bad, taking a moment to think before acting can help you prevent a lot more than just getting caught. Reflective pauses in communication can make it more interesting and ultimately gratifying.

The main point here is: having meaningful conversations requires deliberate decision-making about whether to talk and when to listen.

Every opportunity to talk or listen to someone presents itself when you approach a conversation with presence. This

understanding might mean the difference between having a lively conversation with friends or coworkers or one that becomes dull. Conscious decisions from participants are necessary for meaningful interactions.

A decision point is reached when choosing when and how to listen or speak in a conversational flow.

Therefore, how can you spot turning points in conversations? I suppose with some practice.

Gaining a deeper knowledge of who you are by concentrating on how communication flows for you is the first step. Pick someone in your life with whom you feel comfortable beginning to do that. This is significant since you will be more at ease speaking with them.

Pay attention to when you choose to talk during your interaction with this person. If you realize you've started a monologue that you didn't intend to, stop it. Try coming to a complete stop and giving the other person a little room to leap in. Additionally, you might notice that sometimes you'll feel compelled to speak up and other times you'll feel like keeping quiet. As the conversation progresses, pay close attention to how it feels to actively choose to talk rather than speak without first giving it any thought.

Putting this investigation of your inclinations and patterns into practice will put you on the road to a more genuine kind of expression.

The wonderful thing about communication is that there is no one proper way to engage; instead, it's all about finding a style that suits you. You may have more of the fascinating conversations that make speaking with others such a delight by learning when to speak and when to listen.

CHAPTER 4:

RECOGNIZE YOUR COUNTERPRODUCTIVE CONFLICT BEHAVIORS AND AVOID BLAMING OTHERS.

Have you ever shared a home with a messy person? Imagine cleaning the kitchen for hours only to discover a growing stack of dirty dishes clogging the sink. Because of your aggravation, you might even inquire aloud why your housemate is such a slob!

Do you, on the other hand, view your housemate as a neat freak who always asks, "Why can't you simply relax?" in response to his criticism?

If you take a step back, you'll see that, regardless of which side you're on, your analysis of the disagreement will frequently boil down to what the other party is doing incorrectly. This is because when things don't go our way, we frequently find ourselves blaming others rather than taking responsibility for our part in the conflict.

The main point here is: To recognize your counterproductive conflict behaviors and avoid assigning blame.

When we respond without thinking, we tend to place blame, which only serves to escalate the argument. After all, pointing out your flaws won't likely make you change your conduct if I want you to. You'll only become defensive.

Sadly, we've all acquired a few unproductive conflict resolution techniques. The good news is that by identifying these patterns and then swapping them out for others that would encourage more fruitful conversations, we can modify them.

There are four basic destructive conflict behaviors; Identify your's and change it.

Avoidance of conflict: As the term implies, it occurs when you make every effort to avoid conflict, whether by bringing up a different topic each time one arises or by simply ignoring it.

Conflict between rival groups: That's when we tenaciously pursue our goals while entirely dismissing the view points of others. You can do this by demanding something, yelling at someone, or even threatening them.

Passivity: It happens when we stop before we've even begun, give in to what the other person wants, ignore our needs, and fail to voice our opinions.

Passive aggression: This is a subversive sort of conflict. As the term suggests, it occurs when a scathing, hostile remark is generally hidden beneath a seemingly harmless, or passive, response. Although this type of conflict may appear to be avoidance, it is truly active but not overly so. This can be demonstrated by washing all the dishes except your housemate's to convey a message.

CHAPTER 5:

INTENTION IS CONVERSATION'S MOST POTENT COMPONENT.

A difference of view isn't always a bad thing, even if conflicts can be a painful spot in our communication. It's possible to achieve a deeper level of closeness by amicably resolving a serious conflict with a significant other or close friend.

Because of our uniqueness, life is so rich. They bring us together and aid in our mutual understanding. But how do we ensure that our disputes result in new perspectives and ideas rather than a fight?

Intention is the key to the solution.

The main point here is: the most potent component of dialogue is intention.

The intention behind what we say matters when it comes to communicating. Genuine relationships can be made with people if we approach the situation with the appropriate attitude rather than fall into our old patterns of blaming.

But what does this mean?

Examine your approach to experience. Right, you make an effort to avoid unpleasant things and cling to pleasant things. It's a very organic approach to living your life. Every event is evaluated as good or bad by our minds, which also attempts to prolong pleasurable experiences by avoiding unpleasant ones. When that fails, you frequently end up getting upset at yourself or other people.

But have you ever considered how much energy it takes to seek pleasure and avoid suffering?Trying to manage our experience in this way can soon become aggravating and draining, especially when these factors are out of our control, like another person's behavior.

Thankfully, there is another option. We can simply try to comprehend instead of judging and controlling our experiences. And it is the essence of altering our intentions.

Then how does that operate? Two words best describe the solution: curiosity and care.

Let's talk about curiosities. This emotion is typically brought on by a desire to learn more and an awareness of the gaps in our knowledge. You can quell your curiosity about everything brought up in a discussion or while reading an email by asking yourself two questions: "What matters to me or the other person in this situation?" What can I take away from this?

This strategy can cause a gradual change from drawing judgments right away to merely wanting to know more. You'll notice that your communication improves if you do that. Everyone reacts more favorably to questions than to accusations, after all.

The second word is care. This can be summed up as a willingness to listen and friendliness. It entails beginning with the notion that the other person has something worthwhile to offer. You commit to honoring that once you recognize him as a worthwhile human being with needs of his own that must be taken into account.

CHAPTER 6:

WE STAY ENGAGED IN A CONVERSATION BY LISTENING.

I'm not being listened to by you.

Have you ever heard or said those words during a contentious debate?

The answer is likely yes if you're like the majority of individuals. We've all experienced those discouraging conversations where nothing we say seems to make any sense. Both sides stack arguments on arguments and statements on statements, yet neither side seems to comprehend or even accept the other's point of view.

It's as if we're communicating in separate languages.

That indicates without a doubt that the link has been broken at some point along the line.

The main point here is: listening is how we keep a discussion going.

It usually means that the other person doesn't feel heard or understood when they say we're not listening. A demand for empathy is frequently made.

Therefore, how can you make them feel heard?

A reflective tool is a straightforward tool that you can utilize. It's a means to double-check that what you're hearing matches what the other person meant to say. And to accomplish so, you either pose a query or reiterate her remarks on your terms. By doing that, you allow your opponent to clarify whether they meant what they said.

This method of communication not only aids in conveying the intended message but also fosters an atmosphere of empathy, which can be the difference between a civil conversation and a heated argument.

Let's use an illustration to demonstrate how reflection can be used efficiently. Consider a typical argument that a couple might have. I'm so tired of being the only one who ever accomplishes anything around here, one individual could exclaim in frustration. When someone says that to you, you might be inclined to defend yourself right away by saying, "What about those five loads of laundry I did last week?!"Instead of taking that route, attempt to understand your partner's emotions by expressing them in your own words. you may assis by saying something like, "wow you're weary of this, aren't you?".The adjustment immediately moves your argument toward a potentially more fruitful discussion of this or other relationship problems.

It's okay if this kind of reflection doesn't always feel natural. Just a tool. The most important factor is your honesty, since when someone feels heard, they are also more likely to listen. That is how relationships endure.

Dialogue based strategy

Dialogue based strategy

CHAPTER 7:

THE KEY TO EFFECTIVE COMMUNICATION IS BEING ABLE TO IDENTIFY OUR REQUIREMENTS.

What if you could always hear a person's profound core anxieties underneath their words and deeds, regardless of what they said or did? Imagine having a constant sense of what is important to you in any given circumstance.

This level of harmony with others and with yourself doesn't have to be a pipe dream. It is achievable in everyday life, and all it takes is acknowledging your ideals and needs as well as those of other people.

The fundamental principles that guide all of our behaviors are our needs. They are our priority and the reason we value certain things. We are more receptive to hearing others' needs when we have a deeper understanding of our own. And the better we are at anticipating the needs of others, the more chances we have to establish genuine connections.

The maint point here is: the effective communication begins with an understanding of one another's needs.

Basic wants like food and shelter are among them, as are more esoteric demands like creativity and fulfillment. In addition to connections like those with our families or our communities, we also require feelings like respect and trust. But the truth is that all of our needs count, simple or complex.

But it's usually our methods for addressing those needs—not the needs themselves—that come through in our daily encounters. A strategy is simply a particular technique to address a need, and it is sometimes described as something you want, particularly from someone else. A strategy would be to request your immediate attention, for instance. It probably stems from a desire for understanding. Or if I complain about you turning up late every time we meet, this can be about a need for respect.

Simply put, the way we communicate the needs we're attempting to satisfy causes us to engage in conflicts.

Hence, the secret to preventing conflict is to understand the requirements that underlie the methods.

Imagine that you want to take a trip and that you want to do it with your partner and some pals. Despite how romantic this may appear, your sweetheart may prefer a private getaway. If you and your partner solely think about what each of you wants, you can wind up fighting bitterly about the trip and returning home.

However, if you take a step back and think about the motivations behind the tactics in this example, you might discover that, despite your differing approaches, you are both attempting to satisfy the same need for connection and belonging. When you understand what's at stake for each of you and why you want what you want, you can stop being in a win-at-all-costs mindset

and start cooperating to find a win-win solution.

CHAPTER 8:

EMOTIONS ARE SIGNALS THAT ALERT US TO OUR NEEDS.

What would you do if a smoke alarm suddenly went off in your house right now? Would you continue to act in the same manner in the hopes that it would make you wait for the fire to somehow dissipate on its own, or would you begin scanning the area to see if there was a fire somewhere?

Even though the unmistakable beeping sound serves as a clear call to action, it can be challenging to interpret the signals that come from our bodies and minds.

Our emotions are the sources of these signals, and each one of them is attempting to communicate with us. We must learn to interpret the signals our emotions are sending, just as we can act appropriately when the alarm goes off.

The main point here is: emotions serve as alerts to our requirements.

Most people are indoctrinated to believe that emotions are irrational, dangerous, or frightening in many cultures, and they are frequently linked to negative traits like vulnerability or manipulation. As a result, as children, we are frequently taught to repress and disregard our emotions. How often have you heard, for instance, that "nice girls don't get angry" or "guys don't cry"? once, if not more. However, emotions have a purpose. In actuality, they are the primary means through which our bodies and minds communicate with us about our needs. We feel pleased when our needs are addressed. When they're not, negative feelings like despair or rage take over. They can begin to harm rather than improve our lives when we choose not to pay attention to them. For instance, we can act impulsively and hurt our relationships when we are overcome by emotions like rage. Or, on the other hand, we might hold things in out of fear of being overwhelmed. These kinds of unacknowledged feelings can also be detrimental and hinder our ability to communicate with others. They will continue to manifest themselves in our actions, words, tone of voice, and facial expressions

All of these facial expressions might communicate our true feelings to others. A forced grin or an undercurrent of animosity will not only be detected but is also likely to incite others to turn against us. Emotional agility refers to the ability to thoughtfully manage your emotions. This is being able to identify your emotions, coming up with a means to experience them in a balanced way, and expressing them honestly and without attaching any sort of guilt or judgment.

You can be more deliberate about how you choose to participate in conversations as you become more cognizant of your emotions.

CHAPTER 9:

FINDING A MEANS TO FULFILL A NEED IS THE GOAL OF ASKING FOR SOMETHING.

Do you find it difficult to ask for assistance even when you need it? If so, you are not by yourself. Many of us find it simpler to carry a big load by ourselves rather than to confront our fears and discomfort and seek out And that makes sense. We don't want to be a burden on others; instead, we want to respect their right to decline our requests.

Our intentions are good; it's just that sometimes we fail to consider the needs of others. But we frequently forget about our own in the process.

The main point here is: Asking for something involves figuring out a means to fill a need.

Because when we ask for something, we are admitting our reliance on other people. This might seem particularly challenging. We may feel extremely helpless as a result. That's because it leaves room for disappointment and rejection.

However, the need to give and receive is one of our primal urges. When was the last time you held a door for a friend or performed a small act of kindness for them?

Not because you felt you had to, but just because you wanted to. You're feeling great, aren't you?

All of our wants could revolve around taking part in this delight of giving and receiving if we could learn to ask for what we need. When our requirements are not addressed, it is frequent since no one is aware of what we need. A request is a means of communicating your needs and the exact action you want the other person to take to address them. Recall how we discussed strategies. A fantastic way to satisfy a need is to make a request.

So how do you go about asking for what you need?

Clarity is the key to finding the solution. The more specific you are about what you want and why you want it, the easier it is to find a way to make it happen.

The requests you make benefit from having the following three characteristics when it comes to clarity.

A request should be positive to start with. Otherwise put, Don't express what you don't want; rather, say what you do. Second, it needs to be precise. This means that you must make a specific, realistic request. Finally, exercise flexibility. Make it more of a suggestion, leaving room for various options rather than an order.

CHAPTER 10:

IF YOU PAY CLOSE ATTENTION TO EACH PORTION OF THE DIALOGUE, IT WILL FLOW.

Ever spent all night dancing? Then you are aware of how satisfying a conversation may be. The moves can be challenging to learn, just like in a dance, but they seem amazing when you're spinning away with a partner.

You've learned a lot about the steps so far, but let's now speak about how to put them all together.

The main point here is: Dialogue will flow if you pay attention to its part.

The conversation has its own give-and-take rhythms, just like dancing. In actuality, a successful discussion consists of three key components. We can speak our minds, pay close attention, or just sit still and take it all in.

These are the dance's foundational steps. These guidelines can be used to make them happen as gracefully as possible.

Firstly, there is framing. How you set things up is important. Start with a point of commonality; that is what is crucial. By doing this, you foster a sense of cooperation rather than rivalry.

Let's say you wish to discuss an offensive comment your partner made. Start with some common ground rather than launching into the most painful part, "I felt so wounded when you branded me an egoist!" For instance, you may question her about your talk from yesterday and how you two can better comprehend one another's requirements.

When your communication is going well, it's a good idea to monitor its progress. Tracking is useful in this situation. Maintaining awareness of both the conversation's procedure and the topic is necessary.

To start, be aware of the type of conversation you're having. Are you trying to resolve a logistical issue or is your relationship at stake because you skipped her office party? It's crucial to determine whether the issue is merely one of the scheduling

conflicts or whether there is a more serious interpersonal problem at play, such as her need for assistance.

Another thing to keep track of is who is receiving the most attention at any particular time. In other words, how does the floor pass from one speaker to the next? The more you're conscious of those changes, the more you can do to ensure that everybody has a chance to express their needs.

The talk starts to flow at that point.

FINAL SUMMARY

THIS BLINK'S MOST IMPORTANT MESSAGE IS:

Even though communication is a skill that anybody can learn, it can be challenging at times. It boils down to developing presence, being deliberate about when to talk, mastering the art of deep listening, and being aware of our needs and emotions. We can practice the procedures that result in genuinely satisfying and useful discussions when we genuinely want to connect.

USEFUL

SUGGESTIONS

Take a moment.

Find a clever method to pause the next time you feel overwhelmed during a conversation. Share that you need a break while also making it apparent that you want to stay in touch with the other person. You could, for instance, remark, "I just need a moment to organize my thoughts."